SUSAN BROUGHER

The Strongest Bond
A MEMOIR

outskirtspress

The opinions expressed in this manuscript are solely the opinions of the author and do not represent the opinions or thoughts of the publisher. The author has represented and warranted full ownership and/or legal right to publish all the materials in this book.

The Strongest Bond
A Memoir
All Rights Reserved.
Copyright © 2014 Susan Brougher
v2.0

Cover Photo © 2014 JupiterImages Corporation. All rights reserved - used with permission.

This book may not be reproduced, transmitted, or stored in whole or in part by any means, including graphic, electronic, or mechanical without the express written consent of the publisher except in the case of brief quotations embodied in critical articles and reviews.

Outskirts Press, Inc.
http://www.outskirtspress.com

ISBN: 978-1-4787-2510-7

Outskirts Press and the "OP" logo are trademarks belonging to Outskirts Press, Inc.

PRINTED IN THE UNITED STATES OF AMERICA

Dedication

To my sister, Ellie, I love you.
We learned from each other as we grew our separate ways,
coming of age without a mother to guide us.

THE STRONGEST BOND
A memoir

Everything changes when you're a teenage girl, and your mother dies. The loneliness never stops. You hold on to what once was, and will never be again.

"I think that if I go outside into the quiet of this night, her voice will whisper on the wind, her face will be in the shadow of the moon, and I will remember her, and she will see me looking up."

Susan Brougher

ACKNOWLEDGEMENTS

Thank you, Jim, my husband; you are my constant encourager, my wise and faithful listener. Without your love, and your willingness to stop whatever you were doing, to hear over and over again the words of this book being read out loud, I could not have come this far.

Thank you Works in Progress (WIP), my Somerset, Pennsylvania writing group: Sarene Friedman, Evelyn Morgan, Anne Wood, Kathie Buchanan, Dale Worcester, Ken Davis, and John Rogers. You were the steering force, and the solid ground beneath my feet that kept me moving forward. Your unique writing skills and kind, insightful critiques helped me to believe that I could complete this, my first book.

CONTENTS

1	Changing Seasons	1
2	A Love Story	7
3	A Volcano	13
4	A Triple-Braided-Bond	19
5	Broken Hearts	25
6	Alone	33
7	Dreams	41
8	A Boxing Bond	49
9	A Master Plan	59
10	Wings	65
	Epilogue	71

My mother taught me to safeguard my life force like a lilac beneath the snow that waits until the time is right to bring forth its unforgettable bouquet.

1

CHANGING SEASONS

I asked the memory-keeper, "Can you help me hear my mother's voice and see her face when I was young before she died?" Her reply was kind. As her mouth formed the word "no," she hugged me and said, "Those memories belong to you alone. In the quiet before you sleep, listen for your mother's voice—and when you hear her speak, you will see her face.

IT HAS BEEN MANY YEARS since my mother died, yet without warning a knot comes to my throat and tears fall in an open stream. An overwhelming sense of loss mixes with a still deeper sense of longing. I recall the things we did, but when I try to summon the details, they run away as if I'm counting to one hundred in a game of hide-and-seek.

Growing up, I was a quiet brown-eyed girl with auburn hair and a frail frame. My brown eyes told everything before I opened my mouth to speak. My auburn hair has turned pure white, but the thickness has remained like when I was a child. Not so quiet now and not so frail, I have kept step with the years and aged with a grace for which I am grateful.

WINTER

The wind is a biting cold and raw this day in December. I am helping to bring clothes in from outside and hanging more on the line. My mother's hands are rough and bleeding, but she doesn't seem to mind. Her head is covered with a tight woven babushka, and I am in my pink and white snow hat with matching mittens. I hand the clothes and the pins up as she fastens them with a quick firm squeak. She helps me drag the big bushel basket of clothes across the ground as we go. I gush, asking, "Mommy, why don't you wear mittens like mine to keep your hands warm? I love the snow and this is my favorite chore to do with you."

She answers me with her happy calm voice, "It's too hard to pin the clothes with mittens on. Let's work fast and when I'm done, you can get the lotion for my hands." Her nose is a wind-blown cherry-red. Mine is red too, with snot dripping down to my mouth. I wipe it with my mittens.

We hurry indoors, her carrying the heavy basket, with stiff clothes standing up like people should be in them. As I grab the lotion I tell her, "Put it on quick and feel better." She takes it right away after dropping the heavy basket of stiff clothes to the floor. They smell like outside, fresher than the freshest brisk winds, instantly filling our home, melding with the inside warmth, leaving hints of cool air as a reminder of our time together outdoors. We head to the stove to warm our hands and hold them over our stinging-red cold noses. We laugh about how awfully cold it is.

She promises, "Time for hot cocoa, don't you think?"

Eager and still shivering, I clap my hands and jump with a resounding, head-bobbing "Yes!"

SPRING

My mother had the most delightful lilac bushes that bore light purple blossoms every May. We brought the lilacs in to cast their magic at the center of our dining table each day until there were none left to pick. Their sweet memorable perfume found its way into the corners of our home and settled deep into my sponge-hungry soul.

CHANGING SEASONS

I loved the winter, but I loved spring and the lilacs it brought just as much. The silent snow of winter covered them in a way that said, "Rest a while, so when the time is right you can blanket others with your singular extraordinary aroma." I wished for the lilacs to last and last, but it was as if something so beautiful and sensitive could not live in the reality of changing seasons. Diminutive, they entered through a narrow window in spring, budding into fullness brief in their offering, and then faded, readying for another time, conserving their precious scent.

Many years later when I lived in the South, I longed for the smell of lilacs to enter our home in the way they had when I was young. I saw purple blossoms and ran to suck in the aroma, only to find they looked like lilacs but didn't smell like them. Living in Pennsylvania now, I recently planted lilac bushes. Why I chose paltry twigs instead of bigger bushes, I don't know. I am impatient for the smell of lilacs once again, and the memory of my mother and home. This spring I will buy a large mature lilac tree to capture what my soul desires. I will wait no more.

SUMMER

The air is filled with the scent of cinnamon drifting under my nose as I lean close, watching my mother's hand whisk the spoon around in the big white plastic bowl filled with cinnamon and sugar. Sweet hazy puffs rise and fall, spilling over the edges, just waiting for me to lick my fingers wet to dip the moment my mother looks away. "Can I pour the cinnamon and sugar on, *please?*" I plead. She wipes her brow because it's a hot summer's day for using the oven. I begged so often for cinnamon rolls that she caved in; we all loved them, anyway.

"Yes, I'll give you a cup to dip and pour. Now, remember—no sticking your fingers in the bowl. Can you get me the rolling pin? It's time to flatten the dough."

I watched as she pressed that hunk of dough from the middle out with her big wooden rolling pin. We poured on the sweet mixture and rolled it up like a long thick rope crossing the table. Then she cut it into what looked like tiny bite-sized snails. I waited patiently for those delicious curled-up rolls and when my mother let me test the first one fresh and hot just out of the oven and before supper, as always I declared that it was perfect!

I imagined this was how my mother and I talked when I was young while she baked and I watched, not realizing that before I turned fifteen, she would be gone. Until today I haven't thought much about baking cinnamon rolls the way she did. Her old cookbook is among my most treasured keepsakes, but seldom used; I am not much enthralled by baking like I was before when at my mother's side in the kitchen. At this very moment I am constrained by an urge to leave these thoughts behind and go searching for her recipe.

It is a devious memory that hides my mother's voice and attentive face. Maybe if I bake cinnamon rolls with her recipe while wearing my white apron, she'll come to me in the oven's heat, pulsing aromas into my lungs and through my veins. I bellowed right out loud, "Will I see your face and hear your voice in my kitchen when I bake?" Then I waited in quiet for her to reply.

As clearly as if she were right there, my mother spoke with plain soft words that fell into my ears. "You have never left my thoughts. My voice has echoed and I am sure that you have heard me speak in the rumbling thunder, the dark-blue starry sky at night, the sun at daybreak, the rain and snow upon the ground. I left you in the fall when the leaves came floating off the trees, to clear the way for you to see me looking down at you." She had answered me in nature's style, plaintively aware of how much I needed the outdoors to keep her close and the sadness far away.

The more I sat in silence, the more plainly I heard her speak, and soon her face appeared. It was not pure like an angel, as I'd hoped to see. Instead her features merged into a place far back in my eyes that left a print of *haloed* light. Her presence was long-lasting in spirit, real. So when I heard her say, point-blank, "Get that cookbook out without excuse and make us cinnamon rolls right now," I was reminded of her no-nonsense manner and I celebrated the vision of her sparkling eyes, pulled-up hair and crisp white apron.

FALL

It's hard to say which season I love the most, since nature's changing forms engage my every sense: the quiet sound of falling snow in winter, the fresh after-the-rain scent in spring, the feel of cool mud on my hands patting mud-pies in summer, or the visions of brilliant colored leaves in fall. September is my favorite month. It could be because it brings my birthday, cake, and ice cream. Or that I love summer ending with school beginning. Or that sudden swirling air from every direction makes the noisy rustling leaves seem like creatures approaching. And when I look to see what has startled my imagination, it is the chatter of birds and squirrels traveling on the winds of winter's approach.

The tree's bare branches in fall reveal sights unseen for a while: forgotten houses down the road with smoke rising from chimneys, filling the air with the smells of sweet wood. My heart grows forlorn in this season. I long for what has been, knowing things that have gone before cannot return as they were. And like each season, life moves on in cycles. I am missing my mother's face and the sound of her voice. I think that if I go outside into the quiet of this night, her voice will whisper on the wind, her face will be in the shadow of the moon, and I will remember her and she will see me looking up.

My mother was not afraid of Cupid's arrow when it cut a path of thorns among the roses. Her love was long lasting as symbolized by the carnation. It encouraged me to have no doubt when looking for my soul mate, for clear proof would come as surely as Cupid's arrow, and I would know.

2

A LOVE STORY

I asked Cupid, "Why do you shoot your arrow through a lover's heart? It seems a painful thing to do." He was quick to answer, "True love is not without pain. My arrow pierces like thorns on an enchanting rose that draws the hand to pluck its fragrance mixing pleasure with pain. One lover will hold the other until the pain is gone."

IT IS A COLD THREATENING sky that promises a storm of deep drifting snow and a blizzard for the East Coast. Inside looking out at the yard already blanketed in white, I wait for its approach to sweep in. And wanting to get up to brew a cup of tea, I pause, resisting, intent on placing words long rambling in my head onto a blank white page to soak in the ink of my thoughts.

On the table before me, a picture absorbs my full attention with its pulling force. Thanks to my mother's note at the bottom, I know it is her with my father at Waterworks Park in Michigan, the summer of 1938. Instead of casual sport clothes worn for a day in the park, she is in a floral dress, he in a white shirt and dark slacks.

The expressions on their faces mirror each other with a look of total peace, as if lulled into a place where time slows down and all of life is seen through honey eyes. They sit on the grassy ground, knees folded toward each other, close with their shoulders touching.

Inside her womb, she shelters a new life and the beginning of our family, their first child—my oldest brother, John, due to be born in December. And so this is the chosen image I place at the center of my picture puzzle to balance what I know to be the history of their heartbeats.

Beginning at the young age of seven, I chased boys on the playground, pinned them on the bleachers demanding a kiss, and passed valentines and love notes in class. Where did this crazy love come from? Was it my mother? After all, I am told she fell madly in love with Dad when she moved to Michigan. Much to her family's disappointment, she left the safety and protection of her Pennsylvania home to work in a factory.

Her pioneer life began at about nineteen with my father, six years her senior and more experienced. I imagine her family warned her that taking off with a wild and worldly man who rode motorcycles, and dreamed of owning a gas station, but didn't have a steady job, was no way to enter married life. Not to mention, he'd been on the streets of Detroit since the age of thirteen, when he left home and his abusive father.

His family picture included eight, but unlike my mother's stable household with the same number of siblings, his was shaded with turmoil and uncertainty. She was the love and security he had never known. Standing 5'9", he was a scrappy handsome man with my mother at his side—her facial features strong, a tall slender 5'7" frame. His jet-black wavy hair and deep-blue eyes contrasted with her auburn hair and eyes of the softest brown.

My father's wild yearnings would be quenched by the wooing of my mother in a manner that brought him into the task of raising a family with the best tools he could muster, not ever being shown the way. She, being naive about love and the world outside her home, would doubtless have declared that Cupid's arrow struck so deeply it caused her heart to bleed for only him.

In my forties, I was thinking of writing about how it was for our family losing our mother when we were young. I posed questions to my aunt Hilda, who responded with vague answers and admonishments. She'd say, "Why do you want to write about your life? You kids had it rough. No one wants to hear about it." I didn't understand her then, but she, being very close to Mom, knew the private struggles my mother faced nurturing four young children while taking on most of the responsibility. My mother had relied on affection more than maturity or the comfort of a stable income to live out her test of true love.

As I peruse pictures in forgotten scrapbooks dragged out from an old trunk, my nostrils suffer an assault of dust-gathered particles and musty smells. Laid on a plastic cloth and scattered across my dining table, my first chosen image of them with honey eyes already sits in the middle. It is calling out pictures to circle and settle into a frame so the story can begin.

I start at top left by placing a photo of my mother with her sister Hilda, and two other girls similar in age sitting in a rowboat at the shore with boats to either side. The writing beneath the picture tells me it's Rocky Glen, PA, 1935, maybe just prior to Mom meeting Dad. They show off their classy sundresses as they lean near to each other with laughing smiles.

My second photo fits in the top right frame of my puzzle. It is of my slender mother standing in front of a house with three girls younger than she, close to teenage. My mother's hair is pulled up as it falls across one side of her forehead, her dress long-sleeved with a rounded collar. She wears chic open-toed heels with a strap up the middle. It is Belvidere, Michigan 1937. Could this be my father's family? I have no way of knowing. They didn't visit us, and we went to Michigan only once to meet Grandpa. My father's family was estranged, while we saw my mother's family time and again, since they lived near Plymouth, PA where my mom grew up, and it was closer to where our family eventually settled in New York State.

THE STRONGEST BOND

I frame in the bottom left of my puzzle with a photograph of my mother sitting in a rocker on the porch of a small house with her older sister, my aunt Kate. Upon enlarging this picture dated September 1944, the street address is unmistakable and from other notes about the same house I know it is in Detroit, Michigan. With Google's help, I zoomed in on it and walked the street in front. Emotions welled up as I peered into a home I'd never known and into a stage in my parents' life before I joined the family three years later in Kingston, PA, 1947. My sister, Ellie, would complete our family in 1949.

When this photograph was taken in 1944, my brother John was six. My brother Art would arrive in May of 1945 and live in the same house. Through a real estate search, I found that this house built in 1942 was new to them, with a spacious living area of 425 square feet. The building was more modern, but not unlike the space our family of six, including Mom and Dad, later shared in 1952.

I complete my puzzle frame at the bottom right with a picture of our family standing together in front of a 1949 Pontiac. We wear church-like attire, looking more sophisticated than our lifestyle would have suggested. My father and brothers sport their dress-white shirts and dark slacks. Mom and I wear our printed dresses and Ellie, at about one and half years old, shows off a pretty dress and a determination to escape the tight hold of my mother's arm. Everyone is groomed with poise, our hair parted and combed in place. This is a reflection of my mother's upbringing in a hard-working family of modest means that attended church and pursued occupations in business and education.

I stand looking over the puzzle frame, wondering what other surprises await under my pile of photographs. Will they reveal what has long been stashed away? My frame is set with its four corner points. They are the bones of the skeleton, strong, surrounding the center where it all began when their two hearts joined, willing to hold on to each other, delighting in the aroma of the roses while enduring the stabbing of the thorns.

Allowed this glimpse back in time, I could see the beginning; yet the power of the story lies somewhere in between. I move it forward with remembrances I've lined up for myself: a portrait, a reflection. My mother and father's expressions mirror each other while these words bounce off the page in an attempt to generate a light to help others to understand their own past journeys.

I remember being twelve and dreaming of Prince Charming, but I got caught up in the thorns and roses of real life when my mother was diagnosed with cancer. Our family unit entered into a passage that left us two years later with an empty seat at the table. She was the biggest chunk of love we ever knew. We morphed into an ominous form that drew a spinning mesh of disillusionment over the pictures of our lives.

I gleaned my mother and father's love story from photos, dates, and places, past conversations, and from my sister still here to share her recollections. Yet most important, and not as easy to define, are the memories left imprinted. My heart beats to the tune of theirs, knowing they were where I came from, where my story arose, and yet remains unfolding.

My mother was forgiving and a true reflection of the bleeding heart flower. She suffered the most helpless and egregious emotions; nonetheless, with her love, she balanced my father's painful raging and our fears. She taught me to let go of the burden of hurtful memories, leaving room for only love.

3

A VOLCANO

I asked the student of volcanos, "How do you know when a volcano will erupt?" He placed his hand to his chin in consternation and replied, "We read the rumbling deep beneath the ground and heed the signs, but the exact moment may not be known, and so we watch and wait."

MY MOTHER BECAME LESS AND less the vibrant central figure of our family in 1960 when she began to battle cancer. In those days, it was a disease that little was known about. Not only did it require an opening of her belly to diagnose it, but her own brothers and sisters, thinking cancer was a virus, feared they would catch it when they visited her in the hospital. Sadly, this thinking kept them at a withholding distance that limited the very thing most needed for all of them: warmth and affection. Fortunately, though, our own family embraced her with boundless frequency. Our loss increased in greatness as her illness took more of her away from us, out of the center of our home and into her bedroom where she watched from the sidelines, benched in the game of life.

When we moved in 1952, our new home consisted of a small front porch and one large living room. The tiny red and white wood-frame building stood proudly, placed back from the dirt road in a wide-open yard. Located in nature's setting, it was draped with fields and trees and surrounded by endless deep thick woods, wild berry bushes, and a flowing stream.

On one side of our home a big barn stood with a cooler for storage nearby. On the other side was an outhouse a short distance up a hill near an old open stone foundation that long ago had been abandoned by the house that stood over it.

I was five and starting kindergarten. My sister, Ellie, the baby in the family, was three. Art, my youngest brother, was seven, and my other brother, John, was fourteen. Unbelievably, we fit just fine in that one not-so-big living area, and experienced the true meaning of being a close family.

Our home's one large living room served as dining room, kitchen, and bedroom, with bunk beds against the walls. Our "doll house," as kids on the school bus called it, eventually expanded with added comforts. We'd acquired indoor bathroom plumbing and cold running water, but my brothers continued to haul drinking water in buckets from a spring-fed well across the road.

My sister and I shared a bedroom off the kitchen while my brothers were in a back room entered by going through Mom and Dad's bedroom off the kitchen's other side. In the spring, with our bedroom window open, my sister and I slept listening to the evening crickets chirping, and awakened to the stream's bubbling call and morning birds in song.

At one end of our dining area a tall wood-and coal-burning furnace blasted the heat into our small home. Amazingly, it kept us warm over the cold and snowy upstate New York winters—warm being defined as not cold, and it involved a thin layer of ice on our bedroom floor when temperatures outside hovered near freezing.

Before being connected to indoor plumbing, we employed a white porcelain "pee pail" which we dutifully emptied rather than venturing to the outhouse during cold winter nights. In the warmer months, I'd trek to the outhouse clad in my long granny nightgown. On one of those early-morning visits, while half-awake I opened the door and lifted my nightgown to take my place over the hole in the wooden seat when I spotted the biggest, fattest, stretched-out snake lying lazily against the back wall. I ran in a frenzied state to the house to tell my parents. My father got a big stick and nudged the snake out and back into the field. Before this, I thought nothing of using the outhouse. For a long time afterward, I'd take a flashlight with me in cautious approach to examine every nook and cranny of that place before sitting down.

It wasn't uncommon to see snakes. We grew up in a wilderness playground of endless encounters with the natural elements. We ran barefoot just about everywhere without concern about reptiles, spiders, bees, or any other ground critters.

My mother, a housekeeper for very wealthy clients, and my father, a mechanic for a car dealer in the city, came home each evening from their demanding days at work. If they were tired or grumpy, it didn't show. When we were old enough to be alone for a short while, we'd arrive on the school bus an hour before my parents.

Those days were the good stretches in our life. We ate our supper together, laughed, and talked about school. My sister and I helped with meals, set the table, and later washed and dried dishes. This was how it was for me, at twelve years old, before my world turned upside-down, disrupting the security I'd known.

After becoming ill, Mom was able to spend more of her time at home than in the hospital. She continued to be part of our family activities over the two years of her illness. Dad learned how to take care of her needs after the radiation and drugs murdered her insides beyond repair. We children helped to comfort her with pillow-propping, hair-fussing, and stories about all sorts of things at school, home, and play.

She lingered, alert to all of our comings and goings, until a distant remoteness forced itself upon her. It slowly eroded her ability to join us as we went about, tiptoeing around the prevailing stress fractures in our family unit. She was relegated to the bedroom where she could see and hear us, but could not rise to sit at the table. The evening meals once spent with talk about our days at school flavored with Mom's homemade food, Dad's silly jokes, and my sister and I in giggle fits were a thing of the past, never to return.

Dad took over the meal preparation with my sister's and my help. Mom's empty seat at the table filled our hearts with unmentionable sadness. My father started to exhibit serious signs of inability to cope. His angry outbursts came with an unpredictable force, spewing out like a volcano with fire darting in every direction, hitting either my sister or me for some wrongdoing.

We believed our evening meal gatherings provoked my father's pain. Remembering the happy times lost forever brought up rage in him that boiled to the top like a pressure valve released on a cooker, spewing hot steam on its closest victims.

One evening, my sister and I were joking with each other at supper when I dropped a dish. It sent my father into a sudden wrathful fury. Grabbing my shirt and forcing me against the wall with one hand, and with the other hand wielding a cast iron frying pan, he threatened to smash my head; his red, hot, tormented face was eye-level with mine. Angry shivers of fear raced up my spine. I sorely wanted to strike him down, even with my feet off the floor.

I was skinny, nervous, and fearful—yet I wanted to fight back. But because I was not given to anger by nature, I dealt with my feelings by conveniently stuffing them down inside so deep that to this day I cannot find them.

My distressed mother, lying helpless in the next room yelled as loudly as possible, "Howard, Howard, leave her alone—she's just a child. Please, please stop—don't hurt her!"

Miraculously, my father lowered his threatening stance at the sound of her voice, almost as if taken out of an overpowering trance. In slow motion, he let go of me and put down the frying pan. Without a word he returned to the business of eating with us at the table. My stomach juices, so mixed with fear of my father and hopelessness over my mother, caused my food to barely pass my palate. I'd lost my appetite and hoped I would not be yelled at for leaving my plate half-full.

Later, when I'd kiss Mom goodnight and I guess Dad was out in the barn, she would say, "He didn't mean it. He loves you; you know that. It's just too much for him. I am so sorry."

I would nod my head in agreement. "I know, Mom, but I hate it and I hate him. I don't understand why he picks on me. I'm afraid."

Eventually, when my father returned from outside, his face would be drained of the red flushing, his look woeful, his head tipped downward. Just before settling into bed at night he'd say, "I was upset. I don't know why I did it. It's not you. Do you forgive your daddy?"

I would answer, "Yes, I know you didn't mean it. It's all right." And that would be it until the next time a similar darting fire would come out and attack me or my sister with little provocation on our part. It created in me a fearful state. I searched a way to detect when his violent outbursts would strike. I got good at reading the signs. I had to. It was a matter of survival.

My mother was the loveliest person, a true reflection of her name, Rose, the most fragrant of garden flowers. She taught me to love and accept myself and the beauty within me.

A VOLCANO

pan. Without a word he returned to the business of eating with us at the table. My stomach juices, so mixed with fear of my father and hopelessness over my mother, caused my food to barely pass my palate. I'd lost my appetite and hoped I would not be yelled at for leaving my plate half-full.

Later, when I'd kiss Mom goodnight and I guess Dad was out in the barn, she would say, "He didn't mean it. He loves you; you know that. It's just too much for him. I am so sorry."

I would nod my head in agreement. "I know, Mom, but I hate it and I hate him. I don't understand why he picks on me. I'm afraid."

Eventually, when my father returned from outside, his face would be drained of the red flushing, his look woeful, his head tipped downward. Just before settling into bed at night he'd say, "I was upset. I don't know why I did it. It's not you. Do you forgive your daddy?"

I would answer, "Yes, I know you didn't mean it. It's all right." And that would be it until the next time a similar darting fire would come out and attack me or my sister with little provocation on our part. It created in me a fearful state. I searched a way to detect when his violent outbursts would strike. I got good at reading the signs. I had to. It was a matter of survival.

My mother was the loveliest person, a true reflection of her name, Rose, the most fragrant of garden flowers. She taught me to love and accept myself and the beauty within me.

4

A TRIPLE-BRAIDED-BOND

I asked the weaver of braids, "How strong is the strongest bond?" The weaver looped one piece of cloth into the other and smiled at me. "Ask your heart," he replied. "It knows the answer your mind cannot divine."

IT IS A SNOWY WINTER'S day with loud churning gusts and flying snowflakes accumulating, fast covering the green earth. Wind chimes play a song in harmony with the swaying branches of the tall pine trees. It is a time for quiet reflection. Snuggled inside looking out, I sip hot cocoa while reading a good book, safe and warm in my home.

I stare at one of the few pictures I have of my mother and me. Her love grabs hold of my waiting heart, refusing to let it go. Every fiber in her seems to pull me closer into her mesmerizing gaze. Her love permeates through the framed glass, taking root. Through all storms its invisible protective shield circles me in a gentle embrace. It ignores the fact that we were together only fourteen years. It doesn't care that I have lived nineteen years beyond her forty-six. It lives longer than all space and time, past all physical realms. More than never-ending, it is omnipresent.

In the picture, I am two years old and she is thirty-two. My dark eyes, sad look, and pouting lips stare at the long-suffering picture taker. I restrain a loud cry of protest, wanting to be outdoors at play. My one-piece snowsuit covers all but my face, with a zipper tight under my chin, and a hood over my head. My mother, bent close behind me, places her hand with a light touch on the front of my shoulder. Her dress is print with small flowers, and her hair is pulled up. She wears no earrings. She is neat and prim without fuss or pretense.

Her expression of affection toward me demands all-encompassing words to reveal it. They escape my mind, going straight to my heart with a lovely tug. It is a look of completeness and serenity, a *triple-braided-bond* that none can break. She is my mother, Rose, and I am her daughter, Susan. She loves me more than anything.

When I was seven years old, I wanted to wear long curls. My mother wrapped and looped each swathe of my thick brown hair in old rag strips. Then after a time she'd pull each one free, beam at me, and say, "What a pretty girl you are!" I'd laugh, flip up my hair, and run in circles... for she made me feel so beautiful.

From a very young age I was frail, and illness, especially in the winter, meant a nagging incessant cough accompanied by aching joints. I would be so weak, I'd require a day or two resting in bed to recover. My mother would rub Vicks on my chest. After warming a flannel rag by hanging it over the stove, she'd wrap it loosely across my shoulders and around my neck. "Now isn't that better?" she'd ask. And it would be in an instant. She'd tuck my covers, kiss me on the forehead and quietly leave, saying, "Sleep well, my Susie, and in the morning we'll have hot cereal—just you and me."

With my mother's love and wise home remedies, we didn't need the doctor or the hospital to get better. As it turned out, she really didn't either when she became ill with cancer. We surrounded her at home with the genuine healing of loving hugs and comforting hands—something no hospital or doctor could provide.

When I was eight, my mother sewed my sister Ellie and me matching pinafore dresses of teal blue and silky white to wear for our cousin's wedding. All the guests would be garbed in their Sunday best outfits, and other girls, no doubt, in store-bought dresses and shoes. We had new frilly white ankle socks. They went with our little black patent-leather shoes that were scuffed hand-me-downs until my mother took Vaseline and an old piece of rag, rubbed it in, and together we polished them to a shine.

In the church basement, a long hall of tables filled with food and drink lined the walls around a shiny wood floor. The smells of hot coffee served with dessert lifted spirits and moved almost everyone from their seats, leaping to polka music—and of course, the chicken dance. Ellie and I took to the floor, spinning around dancing unaware that we were any different in our homemade outfits and hand-me-down shoes. In fact, we thought we were prettier than the other girls, all thanks to my mother's creative talents.

Over the years I've seen in myself my mother's inventive "make it work" spirit. If I had those old rags today, I'd weave them into a triple braid, display them in a place of honor in my home, touch them often, and remember.

It happened on September 20, 1962. What started two years earlier with its unrelenting tortures of then-modern medicine's attempt to treat cancer, was finished. My mother's escape from suffering came as a great relief for her and for us—especially Dad, who hated to see her suffer and loved her more than his own life. He was the one beside her in their bed, near to her pain, her decay, her loss of vitality and dignity. He did what he could to lessen the ravages of her brokenness. Their love was the real thing: imperfect, but of a measure not seen in any movie, not comprehended unless you've lived it. A teenager then, I didn't understand that kind of love. It's taken me a lifetime of experiences to begin to grasp its magnitude.

Her dying did not mean she was completely gone from us. In fact, her presence became stronger. We wished with all our hearts, each with our own set of needs, that she could have stayed well and with us forever.

THE STRONGEST BOND

The school year just beginning, I sat in 10th grade art class in the front row on the Thursday morning after our last visit to Mom. Someone came to the door and motioned to the teacher. They spoke briefly, and then the teacher came to me and in a hushed whisper requested that I come with her. Without so much as a word, the person at the door took me to meet my sister and my brother, who had also been called out of class to wait in the school lobby. I don't recall if we were told then, but we knew.

The week before, our family had gathered around my mother's sickbed in General Hospital. Dad stood at the foot; my sister, my two brothers, and I bordered her on one side as we sat in reverent silence on sterile straight-backed chairs. The four-bed ward's big windows shed a welcome warm light across the room; a space down the middle separated two beds on either side facing each other. Mom was to the right and near the window, her frail body covered by a thin light sheet and white blanket that exposed the outline of her emaciated frame. Her head rested motionless centered on a soft pillow, her hair brown and wispy, and her eyes dark and sunken.

After a short time, Dad said, "Kiss your mother goodbye. She needs to sleep; we should go home now."

In turn, we each approached her bed and bent to say goodbye. "I love you, Mom," I said. And, as if her arms were made of the heaviest lead, they lay at her side immovable, unable to reach out and hold me. Robbed of what we both yearned for, her breath remained upon me as she planted her lips on my cheek and I returned her kiss. She smelled of Ivory soap; she smelled like home.

In a low soft voice, every word a breathing effort, she said, "I love you, my Susie. Take care of your father. He needs you. Love each other."

My mother had a sense of joy within her like the delightful Sweet William flower that grants wishes and allows for play. It reached out to us as we journeyed on our individual paths to find healing from the inside out for our broken hearts.

5

BROKEN HEARTS

I asked a cardiologist if he could mend a broken heart. He replied in a clinical tone, "I diagnose the damage and order medication, or if the blood flow is blocked a surgeon can repair the arteries. But when love breaks a heart, it cannot be fixed from outside in; it must find a path to heal from the inside out."

SPRING ARRIVED A FEW DAYS ago without a reprieve from winter's grip. It brought a cold wind with a tiny hint of warm air behind it, the distant sounds of birds singing, and fat red-breasted robins bouncing over hard grass-patched ground. The month of March is meant to usher in a season of new growth, blue skies, green trees, warm breezes, and hope.

The month of September, unlike March, carries the promise of colored leaves, crisp air, and a final burst of activity as it prepares for going inside to the silence when winter's snowy cover descends.

When my mother died just before my fifteenth birthday, her family helped as best they knew how. During the week of, and for a few weeks following my mother's funeral, our family gatherings were busy and I was happy to have friends and relatives visit. My cousin, a common "city slicker," surprised us by getting up on our pony, Peanuts, and riding him around the yard, coaxing the pony and wearing a cowboy hat. The extra activities were dreamlike and went by quickly. At first, I didn't notice that my mother was gone for good.

THE STRONGEST BOND

Thoughts of summer storms, falling rain, and lightning bugs remind me of when I was about seven years old and a horrific thunderstorm with hurricane winds blustered through. From our tiny two-room house in a wide open field, we could see bolts of lightning piercing straight into the hilltop across the road. Its white fury against the purple sky, with fast-moving clouds and searing rain, lit up the landscape. The terrifying howling winds, the booms and rumbles of thunder shook the dining table as our family sat huddled beneath it against the wall, a framed print of The Last Supper hanging steadfastly over us.

And as scary as that storm was, after a few days my sister and I were found running barefoot, scantily clothed, dancing and squealing as raindrops fell over us and into our gaping mouths, giving us a drink of relief from the heat.

In the summer, lightning bugs floated over our grassy fields in abundance. They captivated us as we ran with our glass canning jars, holes punched in the lids, chasing their elusive luminous bodies. We couldn't wait to get into bed and watch them glow like a flashlight under our sheets.

In the quiet and in the stormy times, my mother had been my help and strength, the one who took my side and listened to my story. She saw the real me, and when I talked to her she made me feel important, never requiring that I worry about her, even in her sickest days at home.

I did worry about her, though. She'd cared for me during the two years of her illness, not thinking of her own needs. In the summer I'd sit at her bedside just to be near her, and I'd feel guilty about going out to play with neighborhood friends. I'd say, "I'll stay with you today Mom, because if I go outside, you'll be lonely. And what if you need a drink or something? Who will get it for you?"

Then she'd say, "I'm fine. I'll be napping. Besides, you can come back and check on me, can't you?"

I'd come back, if only for a short time to spout about the games we were playing, to give her a drink, to fix her covers or to comb her hair. Somehow her words allowed me to go, to be a child, to play freely and still be with her to help. During those days, I was learning to balance what would be the future nurse in me: willing to bring all of myself to the bedside, yet able to leave the suffering behind when I needed to nourish my own soul.

After Mom died, my father became remote, growing away from the family, despondent one minute and angry beyond his own recognition the next. It seemed like he would have done anything to keep things the way they were before my mother got sick. As unfathomable as it was, I remember my out-of-control hormones making me feel that in a blink he would have traded my life to keep my mother's. But I knew better because he would say, "I pick on you the most because I love you so much. You're sweet and kind like your mother." I sensed his hurt and misplaced blame, the hateful anger that he directed at himself—and on occasion at us, after too much alcohol.

How did I get up, get dressed, and go back to school that September of 1962 without her? I had become more independent during the two years of increased household duties, and by the time I'd turned fifteen it felt like I'd grown up faster than instant coffee. Instead it was more like a slow-roasted drink of sadness, anger, and pain mixed with the sugar of the sweetness of my mother. It was a sweetness that laced everything. It swirled around and came out in my father's ranting. On good days it was stories of horses and the neighborhood kids, and he'd ask about how we were doing at school.

But for the most part he'd lost interest in us—or I should say that his interest was overcome by intense feelings of guilt and an overwhelming sense of responsibility. Running the household without my mother for support was a task that required a résumé of skills he had not acquired.

THE STRONGEST BOND

Our evening meals were silent when Dad was present, which after my mother died, was not often. My oldest brother John, who worked at a Sheltered Workshop for the disabled, would travel home with a neighbor and eat with us in the evening. He lived at home and didn't graduate from high school. Due to his nervous condition and physical ailments, he couldn't drive. He, my other brother, my sister, and I fended for ourselves at home. We girls fixed the meals and cleaned the house. When we all ate together without Dad, we talked about home, school, and friends.

Truthfully, we hoped he would not return during mealtime, since it gave us opportunity to share our feelings, which provided a relief from the stresses and a way to plan for his unpredictable moods. We were never sure if he would offer a hug or drag us from our rooms, where especially my sister and I hid, and demand why the dishes weren't put away in order or the floor wasn't swept or hay wasn't put down like he wanted for the horses.

On his way home from work, he'd stop for maybe just one drink, but it almost always led to another. The liquor made it easier for him to force himself to return to the emptiness of our home without Mom. We'd leave him a plate of food to warm up, hoping he would eat it, which I think most of the time he did, alone in the quiet.

Alcohol took over by filling the terrible draining void that nagged at him from the moment he awoke until his thinking was numbed enough to sleep at night. But the memories would return on each new day with reminders of how it was and never would be again. He wanted my mother back—and instead he had us, with our lack of understanding, and our neediness as children. He didn't have anyone to share his sorrow with; a sorrow that I imagine ate away at him like a worm burrowing a hole into his heart. At least we had each other, but we still needed him to be our father, the father he once had been.

When he did join our evening meals after school, he never

allowed us to talk about anything in our lives before with Mom. It was as if she had never lived: never cared for us, cooked our meals, kept up with our school work, laughed, washed and mended our clothes, and had never done anything that made us a family. He was determined to keep all the memories, all of the pain, and all of her love to himself. We were too young to imagine what it was like for him. We needed to keep our mother's memories alive. He wanted the pain of her dying to be buried along with our memories, and forgotten.

And so, my father, who was already a difficult man to know, grew more distant, creating a wall of anxiety in me along with a conflicting desire to help him feel better. Unfortunately, the anxiety grew stronger while the desire to help him faded away. I had too much sorting-out of my own to do, teenage longings that surged in me without anyone to talk to or encourage me to grow from a timid girl into a confident young lady.

While I was still at home before graduating high school, my father on no occasion talked about another woman, and never brought a lady into our home. In fact, I didn't have anyone like a mother, no adult female or mentor to talk to about teenage things, like "that time of the month," boys, clothes, school, hairstyles, make-up, or how this or that looked, and so on.

My sister, two years younger, would work things out in her own way. She had a sense of style, and girlfriends who drove, enabling her to escape from home with them. But when she was old enough to drive, she had to endure my father's and my brother's exceedingly impatient driving instructions. Getting the car required dogged fighting, yelling, and general household upset, none of which I deemed worth it for me to learn to drive. By the time she was sixteen, she'd taken off when a car was available and seemed to be having fun. This made me feel better about when I would turn eighteen and leave at the first opportunity.

THE STRONGEST BOND

Home ceased to be our haven and was more of a lonely sea where we passed resembling sailing ships in the night. It was like we were searching for direction from a lighthouse perched atop a sturdy rock, hoping the light shooting far across the dark and stormy seas could point us to the safety of shore.

Our family from a distance resembled a marigold flower. We were like indistinct clumps broken by the loss of our mother. Yet on closer inspection, we had begun to gather our nondescript petals to form distinct bold-colored blossoms with a strong protective fragrance.

6

ALONE

My words shot blankly into the air. "Everything is different now—I don't know what to do. Who will help me?" Not expecting a reply, the answer I already knew filled my heart with fear. "You're alone now; it's up to you."

IT WAS AFTER MIDNIGHT. AND like many other nights since Mom had been gone, I couldn't sleep for thinking of her. Pajama-clad, I'd sit in the kitchen chair, with its straight back and padded seat, my knees drawn up to my chin, my arms tightly holding them. Everyone else was sleeping. It was the quietest time. The house was mine: to feel, to think, and to gain strength in being alone with memories and my mother's spirit. I sat at our kitchen table where she and I had prepared meals, and after setting out the dishes we'd go to the door and yell into the open space between the barn and house, "Dinner's ready, come and get it!"

In 1947, I was born, meant to be the one in the middle. My sister, Ellie, entered the world two years later and my brother, Art, was already in the family two years ahead of me. This counted me as a true middle child even though I had another brother, John, nine years my elder. I had the good fortune of birth in September: a fair, balanced, and graceful Libra, according to the stars. These were traits I needed from very early on. My brother Art and my sister Ellie possessed domineering, astute, strong-minded personalities.

I learned that by letting them fight it out I could still get my own way by default without their realizing it and without having to join in the ruckus. When they got what they wanted, I got what I wanted too. And so, as a seemingly shy girl, I developed perceptive people skills with a creative attitude toward life that strengthened my personality and saved me from dips of unhappiness. I was busy making "Plan B's" for almost every situation.

From the beginning of my mother's illness, my sensitivity and introspection became heightened. I searched constantly for signs to grasp the changes in and around me. The family that once held me close and made me feel safe was eroding faster than I could keep up with as I struggled. For a long while after Mom died, the days passed like I was living in a vacuum. I stopped expecting any kind of response or reassurance similar to what my mother would have given me. A terrible loneliness took over. I was forced to figure out the answers and solve problems myself without the benefit of any adult, let alone someone like my mother who could guide me with her own irreplaceable love and wisdom.

My father could not provide support, compliments, or encouragement, or answer questions like "Is it normal to have cramps once a month that hurt so much that I have to curl up in a ball and hold my stomach?" Gaining help from him about my feelings was not something that had occurred before, and it was less so after Mom died.

My search for a rest from upheaval took me on paths walking outdoors with notebook and pen in hand. Into a world of greens and blues I went, quietly watching and waiting for life in the open air to spring into action and overtake my aching thoughts. I'd lean against a tree in the midst of a forest of shrubs, berry bushes, and towering pines. My seat was nature-made with a layer of grass, leaves, and dirt that soaked into my pants with its earthy moss. I'd perch on a sloping hill overlooking the fast-flowing stream below. Waves of flickering sunlight drifted down, moving over my page, and when looking up I could see the clouds moving in and out playing peek-a-boo with the sun.

The wide expanse of heaven over my head and the foundation of ground under my feet gave me solace in the woods. In my writing, my feelings poured out, but it still was not enough. Already naturally quiet, I became more withdrawn and insecure about everything. It was 1962, my tenth year in high school. A gaping hole centered itself in my chest, weakening my body and mind. It was the absence of my mother.

The experience of losing her to death was something that to this day I cannot fully describe. I can't find enough words to match the feelings I hold. I have searched books longing for understanding, but most of all I wanted to hear from someone, "I know what you mean, I felt that way too when my mother died." But in all these years I have not met someone who had similar feelings, who went through the loss of a mother when they were in their teens. I yearned for a sense of commonality to help me heal.

My fears had increased at school more than any other place, almost from the time my mother became sick. I'd lost confidence, and was unsure of how to answer the teacher's questions. A not-so-pleasant memory comes to mind of an experience I had at school right around when my mother became ill. I had to make a speech in the auditorium for my English class. I was so frightened that I could not speak for what seemed like forever. My classmates stared at me and grew restless; some looked worried, some started to laugh at me, and others joined in laughing to relieve the tension. Then I laughed too, not knowing what else to do, unable to gain control, and not able to deliver the presentation I'd planned.

My self-doubts were many and included fear of a wrong answer, being stared at or made fun of, saying something stupid, or not looking right. At lunchtime in school, when waiting in line I worried about leaking through protective pads when I thought I would faint from a light-headedness that came along with that time of the month. In the cafeteria when I had to eat in front of others, my hands would shake, causing my utensils to stab aimlessly at my mouth—so much so that I chose finger foods instead of a meal, to keep from being embarrassed.

I possessed a superficial understanding of my monthly period, from my health classes. I didn't share intimate stuff with my few girlfriends, since I knew them only in school, where there was little time or place for candid conversations. The one talk I had with my mother on this topic had occurred when I was around twelve years of age, just before she became sick. She would unpack groceries and place aside a mysterious brown paper bag that I never got to look into. When I'd ask what it was, she'd say, "Soon you'll be ready for me to tell you all about it." We did discuss it later, and I remember being disappointed yet excited about something my mother held out to me as wonderful.

I felt isolated from other students who could have boosted my self-confidence. Instead, I viewed them as alien. They really didn't recognize what my life was like. They talked about their parents; they dressed in style and weren't afraid to speak up in class. They laughed in the halls and walked in groups, while I walked alone between classes back and forth from my locker for books. I couldn't figure out how to interact with other teens; it was awkward for me in their world, and it was difficult for me to express myself.

On occasion I was allowed to stay overnight at a friend's home, which slightly abated my feelings of separation. My home was so different from theirs. I never felt at ease inviting them to stay over because my house was so tiny, way out in the country, and without modern conveniences or a bedroom of my own.

My friends had stylish clothes instead of hand-me-downs, modern furniture and appliances, big sturdy-framed homes, a bathtub and shower with running water, and a bedroom all to themselves.

Instead of being in awe, I was out of place and afraid that I'd say or do something mistaken around them or their parents. My feelings of disconnection were reinforced, not having a complete family and solid home like they did.

I imagine that I was hard to get to know. The real me was hiding feelings deep, foreign to theirs, protected in my incomprehensible landscape, with only occasional spots of light to allow them a glimpse. When I spoke, my words were guarded, unnatural, soft, and I was hesitant when attention was directed toward me in expectation of a response. I needed the self-assurance of what I could predict to some degree: that being, the social world that existed at home with my siblings.

Fear and insecurity drove many of my actions at school that year, except in places of reprieve when I engaged in team sports and music. In these activities I performed well and wasn't singled out. I felt valued, as I played an important part in a success shared by everyone.

If the other students knew anything about what it was like to go home without a mother to greet them, I was not able to fathom it. All I knew was that when I came home from school, my mother was not there to listen, to care about my day, to encourage me, to give wise advice, or to soothe my adolescent troubles. No one seemed to know a thing about how different it was for me having a gravely ill mother with cancer, and then no mother. I couldn't tell anyone. It seemed like my other classmates lived in a carefree world.

The teachers were distant, not personal with the students. They couldn't help my father or protect me, my sister, and brothers from his increasing remoteness and inward anger. I was lonely, separate, hidden out of sight behind a covering of clouds.

And so all the things that were before, when my mother was healthy, slowly faded away that sophomore year. Our family had flaws but it was once whole: father, mother, and children doing things together, sharing, helping each other. The emptiness that overshadowed our home pushed me deeper inside myself.

I was without my mother to share my life and to tell about the things I desperately wanted her to know: how my day at school went, what happened with my friends, the "A" I got in English, the boy I liked who sat in front of me in class, my dress that didn't fit right, my shoes that were out of style and too tight, the locker combination I was so afraid of forgetting, all the books I had to read in school since we didn't have them at home, the assignments in math that I could not figure out, other girls who wore lipstick and had stylish haircuts, and how inferior I felt. I was not able to measure up, not perfect enough for anyone, not my friends and neighbors or my sister or brothers...and especially not my father, who rarely seemed to notice me.

As strong as my uncertainties grew at school, they subsided somewhat at home. I fought with my sister over washing and drying dishes and fixing the meals, and of course the clothes, always the clothes—even though we had barely enough between us to fill the tiny closet we shared.

My sister and I petitioned our brother Art to drive us to school events. If we were not ready to go when he was, he left without us. That happened only once or twice, since he had the power to transport us to fun and normalcy at school events with other kids. We learned to jump into that car, ready or not. My oldest brother, John, may not have finished high school, but he was the smartest. In his room with his radio and headset, he wisely enjoyed the music of life, literally, and avoided the angst his three teenage siblings thrived on.

Undoubtedly, without a mother we grew closer to each other in our handling of life. Our bond at home helped me to wade through the weeds that surrounded in high school as I continually forced myself to deal with the changed life, the reality I had to get through

ALONE

without my mother. We learned to protect each other, and as we shared our weaknesses and gained harmony, our father moved beyond his weakness into an acceptance of the new nature of our ever-evolving family.

My mother's spirit filtered down through a veil of love, sheltering me, like my favorite pine tree with its sustaining roots, fragrant green limbs, and sturdy trunk. Because of her love, I could dream a million dreams. I could touch that branch in the sky with the tip of my shoe, without needing a swing to take me there.

7

DREAMS

In the summer of 1963, I told my mother, who had died the year before, "One minute I feel like I'm on a swing touching the sky, my feet free, and the next minute, I scuff the ground, unable to pick them up fast enough. I want to stay, up forever touching the sky above, close to you. But when I return to where I started, I'm pulled back into my life. And I'm sad all over again, because you're not here anymore."

I HAVE FOREVER LOVED THE SWAYING motion of a swing, and would jump on the closest one. Recently in a school parking lot while waiting for dark skies and the fireworks to begin, I walked across the field to the swing sets. Thrilled at the chance to feel the breeze at my back and in my face, I jumped in the swing's seat to find it was made for little kids. My small frame scarcely fit on the hard rubber seat between the rusted chains, while my feet held fast to the earth below. My knees were constrained too high for me to back up and push even if I wanted to.

Disappointed, I was denied the feeling I longed to capture once again of being young and carefree, pumping the ropes of that swing. Over the years I've had visions of returning to my old school playground, swinging one more time, higher and higher. I wanted to stretch the tip of my shoe to reach for that tree branch that hung overhead and above my feet as I swung suspended in the open blue sky.

I never wearied of the swings on the playground at school or the old tire swing that hung by a rope from a tree next to my house. Swings took me to the heavens with tickles—laughing, kicking, and dreaming. But when I could no longer push the ground, or pull the ropes, my feet scraped, slowing me down. They brought me back to where I began.

It was as if the world were determined to keep me down—and for what? I asked, that summer when I was almost sixteen. Some days I just wanted to be done with all those things that kept my feet fixed on the ground. I wanted to rise above it all, to find that carefree child I had been, the one before, when I had a mother to fix my meals, kiss me good night, listen to my every plea, and above all, love me like no one else could.

When school was in session, most of our days were taken up with classes. We also played musical instruments: my brother Art, the violin in orchestra; my sister, the clarinet; and I, the flute in band. We were involved in all kinds of sports and intramural activities like tennis, field hockey, basketball, and volleyball as we traveled to other schools. These events meant we often stayed after to ride the late bus home. I was able to spend time with friends one-on-one during the long rides and began to shed my shyness and feelings of isolation.

When we were growing up, on weekends in the summer, my parents had played cards with friends late into the evening; inevitably requesting we perform for their guests. They'd sacrificed the little extra money they had to buy our instruments, and were no doubt proud of our musical talents, such as they were. We'd dutifully obey, and then go outside to join in games with the neighborhood kids and our parents' friends' children.

Late into the night, our fun would seem endless while we stayed up longer than usual, and my mother and father laughed enjoying their respite from long difficult days of work. This flurry of doings with family and friends was one of many types of gatherings that didn't seem to fit without my mother. The couples my parents knew rarely visited after Mom died. The house lulled into a quiet somber sound, as if holding the vibration of our music within its walls, unable to release it into the air without my mother there.

My life had changed beyond what I could have ever believed. I was getting used to how different it was with my sister, brothers, and father when at home in the emptiness without my mother. I missed playing our musical instruments for company, even though we dreaded dragging them out and agonized through the process of making music together.

By some miracle of fate, after finishing a lonely sophomore year in high school, I was asked to work at a Jewish summer camp run by the family of a boy in my class and located just miles from the small town where I attended school. I was surprised when my father, after being cajoled by my favorite aunt Hilda and others of my mother's family, allowed me to leave for six weeks to stay and work at the camp. Each week I called to let everyone back home know how I was doing, but otherwise I was on my own, free, pulling and pumping those swing ropes high into the air, reaching for that distant tree branch.

I worked in the kitchen, made matzoh ball soup and followed the kosher customs in food preparation. As I learned the skill of making matzoh balls float, and not sink, I began to drift above the weighty feelings and responsibilities that had dominated the year before. I cleaned in their house and the recreation hall, and washed and sorted laundry.

There was a young boy, a camp counselor from New York City who followed my actions as closely as I did his. Our eyes would meet, then fall away, waiting, looking for the next glance, infatuated with each other. I washed, dried, and folded his boxer shorts, letting them stay in my hands longer, enjoying a mysterious sensual longing not known to me before.

THE STRONGEST BOND

I had moved beyond innocent talk and giggling with boys. It was not that long ago, in the previous summer, when games of spin-the-bottle brought sudden surges of heat when it stopped and pointed to a certain boy for a kiss. My internal workings ignited in great eagerness. The chemistry of sexual attraction drove my changing body, defied explanation and could not be found in my sex-education books.

One balmy evening near the end of my time away, when stars were abundant in the clear night sky, the boy and I walked hand-in-hand a short distance down the road from camp. My head was full of dreams. I wanted to run away with the wonderful freedom that enveloped me as I wished for the unreal night to never end. I had a happy lightness and excitement about a future that was all mine.

I was almost sixteen, and he was not much older. At a small restaurant just off the road, we sat close while sipping our sodas. We savored each other's presence, the sensations between us of young, pure, sweet love. They were the kinds of feelings that belonged to that time of innocence. They would exit as quickly as they entered with their fresh new excitement that allowed for the process of love to begin its many ways of being.

His arm around my waist, our bodies touched side to side as we went along the road, getting closer to camp and the end of our time together. We dipped briefly into an alcove of trees, for a fleeting moment and a short goodbye kiss.

As we headed back, the moon's face was complete, bright, sending light flooding over the trees, striking the road with the passion of a noonday sun. The sky grew a darker midnight blue, in contrast to the stars now looking like holes in the curtain of heaven. Our moment in this place was over—we would not meet again.

My desires were kindled that summer far from the confines of my home and school demands. The cravings whirled in my head and fiercely settled in my heart. I was not the same girl who had left home six weeks earlier. The images of love and a Prince Charming to take me away to continual bliss magnified. I had not a hint of what this new awareness would bring me. Engulfed in totally escapist power, I thought the lifting mood would carry me through any difficult struggles that waited upon my return home. But the problems I'd left behind piqued all the more while I was gone, and I was now less willing to undergo their torments.

After returning to the routine at home from my respite away, I found the hurtful noise of unhappiness more unbearable than ever. I could find no place to hide when contentious shouting took over our small living space one evening not long after I returned. There was nowhere to be free of it and go back in time to that feeling I had away at camp.

Without any forethought, I steeled myself in the farthest corner and curled into a ball like a baby in the womb. Fighting for protection and fending off the pain, I heard a cacophony of sounds, utterings, erupting from way down deep within me. No words formed from the screeches in my throat as I rocked, huddled against the wall, shielded in my self-conceived barrier from all that surrounded me. I murmured over and over inside my head, "If only Mom was here."

When the quiet came, I slowly unfurled, looking around to confirm that I was indeed alone. The noise was over for now, each family member parted to their own discontent. I made a plan then to leave, to run away. I packed an old pillowcase with provisions and the next day, I left, going early into the woods, before others could detect my absence, fully intending to stay. I would be gone long enough for someone to miss me, someone to care that I wasn't there.

The day wore on. I'd eaten my snacks and thought about supper. The late summer sun was beginning its descent, creeping down a little behind the tall trees; maybe it was six o'clock. No one came looking for me. Didn't they wonder where I was as I sat under my much-loved pine tree with its sheltering bough of green fragrant needles?

The old dead branches beneath the pine formed a roof covering. An earthen floor of cool dirt, roots, leaves, and pine needles rested under my feet. Their strong earthy aromas encircled every part of my being and tucked me away from the rest of the world. Leaning completely against the rough tree bark, at first secure, as the day wore on reminded me of how thin my summer shirt was. I put on my sweatshirt, pulled the hood over my head, and waited. The sun was less warm, the ground more cool; fears that no one cared began to mount.

My resolve to stay away weakened as I sat under nature's homemade roof over my head. I'd had time to recover my strength, to write poems and make plans in my notebook, to listen as the birds sang songs to each other, unknowingly gracing me with their melodies. Maybe the world was not so bad after all—with a few short days left before school, I could begin again. I stood, restored, ready for the joy of learning with its promise of new experiences and fresh ideas to seize my mind. I wanted to return to my school friends, classes, marching band at the football games, sports, and maybe a boyfriend that year.

As I walked back into the house, my sister and brother greeted me like I'd never left. Busy with their own plans that day, it was only near suppertime that they had momentarily pondered where I was. My oldest brother, John, had arrived home from work. We made a quick meal. Dad came home on time, in a good mood that day, and joined us. Maybe it would be all right. Maybe we could mention how much we all missed Mom.

I quickly fell into a sound sleep, drained from the days of readjustment at home. In the middle of the night my eyes unwrapped from slumber to see across the room my mother in her pink quilted robe. We talked as if her presence meant she could stay, but soon

DREAMS

she said she had to leave. I sobbed and my chest began to shake without control. Tears I'd held deep inside over the past year fell down my face and into my pillow as I pleaded, "Will I see you again? I miss you so much."

Her loving words wafted in the air and landed in my soul like soft kisses. "When you need me, remember I am with you, always."

I held the orchid's beauty close, hoping the magic it brought that prom night would bring him back to me. Instead it made me steady and strong for a journey without him. I kept it pressed between waxed paper in a book as a reminder of our special time, wanting never to forget us. I had formed new goals and moved on, sometimes thinking I didn't deserve to be happy.

8

A BOXING BOND

Dear Daddy,

There was a time when I was nine and couldn't sleep. From my bed into the living room I'd come begging, "Please can I stay up and watch TV with you?" I'd get a snack and move my chair to where you were. "I'll be quiet," I would say. You'd look at me and nod, engrossed in the Friday Night Fight. We didn't talk much, sitting close beside each other. I liked it there with you.

The men were punching with padded gloves into each other's face, dancing back and forth in a raised-up ring. People jumped and screamed and so did you, sometimes, with a quick "shush" to yourself. Then to me you'd say, "It's late and everyone else is sleeping."

I cry when I think of the better times before the Friday Night Fights were no more. That phase of you and me went away. We had fights, but they were in the living room, at the center of our lives. I hardly knew who you were then. Instead I chose to remember when we sat together on Friday nights, to watch our favorite boxers fight.

Love forever and always your little girl,
Susie

FINALLY, MY JUNIOR YEAR IN high school had arrived. Naïve, at sixteen years old that September of 1963, I approached the coming year full of hope, with a heart sprinkled in notions left over from my brief summer's romance. I was not capable of knowing that I was becoming a different person right before my eyes when I gazed into that reflection in the mirror.

Family life was changing too. My brother Art had graduated high school and was accepted with scholarship to a college in upstate New York. I was glad for him and for his chance to realize some of his own desires. In a way, he was our defender when Dad was angry. I felt insecure and worried about being without him at home. John, my oldest brother, was timid. He'd become visibly upset whenever arguments ensued and retreat to his room quickly to avoid conflict. On the other hand, Art would confront my father, who most of the time listened to him without fighting back.

On one occasion my father struck out at John, who turned away, flinching in response. It caused Art to swing a connecting fist that landed grazing my father's face. A brief tussle followed with a few blows exchanged as my sister and I yelled for them to stop. Art was tall with brown hair and brown eyes like Mom's, and at a height above six feet he towered over my dad's shorter sturdy muscular frame. I remember feeling we would all gang up on Dad should he ever strike any of us. I believed I could fight to protect myself and my brothers or sister if I had to, even though I weighed only about ninety pounds. We'd always look out for each other.

Fortunately, that episode of physical aggression, although an example of the festering anger my dad held just below the surface, was not indicative of his usual responses. His expressions of anger after my mother died occurred as verbal rampages that did not lead to physical assault. Yet his cursing, name-calling insults and mean accusations directed toward me carried an even more demoralizing effect.

It had been a bumpy ride. Art had carried much of the burden of responsibly in the years before, when Mom was sick, and after she died. He helped Dad to prioritize bills left over from her hospital stays and managed the checking account. He worked hard to tame tempers and stresses that persisted as we weathered life without our mom.

My father placed great expectations on Art, and possibly saw that he could achieve what my father could not. He was proud of his academic success. Conversely, he did not express the same enthusiasm when it came to my sisters and my accomplishments, other than to say, "You don't have to worry about getting an education. You'll find a man to marry and take care of you."

My brother John had a five-day-a-week job in town. His big blue eyes lit up when talking about work, changing his expression from a sometimes sullen appearing young man to a happy individual with wavy blond hair and a paunchy belly. My dad and he would head out early in the morning. And when my father did not return home directly after work, John would catch a ride with a neighbor. My brother found pleasure in his assembly line job and in the people he shared his day with, in spite of being paid low wages. He kept some of the money for his own enjoyment, usually spent on records, and the rest of his paycheck he gladly relinquished to support the running of our household.

My blonde, green-eyed sister's boundless energy and forceful nature settled somewhat. Maybe she missed battling over chores and clothes the previous summer when I was absent. She may have been glad to have me back again, especially with Art planning to leave that year. My quiet accepting energy was in constant conflict with her high-strung personality. But we learned from each other as we grew our separate ways, coming of age without a mother to guide us.

We rode the late bus home from school and had a routine for getting supper ready and doing household chores. When Art went away to college, another sort of loneliness invaded. Dad was home most evenings, and on occasion we talked about Mom. Now the table was set for four. The family living at home was getting smaller. Dad's anger seemed less, but his sadness was palpable as he distanced himself, and remained unpredictable when he drank.

He'd pretty much stopped talking to us following Mom's death, but now was starting to make attempts at conversing, albeit sometimes not to our benefit. It was a delicate balance trying not to say something that upset him. He was going through the motions of listening to my sister, my brother John, and me. Together more often for supper, we were still slowly growing apart.

As I began to develop a more self-determined personality, in my mind I formed my future plans. This idealized thinking fixed impatience in me coupled with the desire to be out of the house and on my own like Art. I was looking for a summer job that could give me money and the freedom to leave after high school. But in accordance with my father's opinion, I also thought that I should find a man to marry.

Distracted by daydreams in class, I stayed determined to finish high school. With Mom gone, my sister and I had no one to encourage us to do well. But I moved on, confident from high grades on written assignments and my musical awards in band. I loved school, yet I was drawn to the idea of being able to do what I wanted without restrictions or obligations.

The family we were the year before was changing as fast as the times in which we lived. It was November 22, 1963, a Friday afternoon. The cool autumn season brought a light-azure sky with sparse floating strings of white clouds and an early out-of-school-day for me. I was feeling poised and pretty, in my box-plaid skirt with knee socks and penny loafers, fortunate to have my cousin's fairly stylish clothes. For the few items that needed repair, we acquired talent working at the Singer treadle sewing machine with my mother. Her instructions gave us the ability to hem, stitch, follow patterns, and sew buttons.

A BOXING BOND

My sister was much better than I was at sewing and following patterns, but not as coordinated. Cringing even now, I recall the day she ran the sewing machine needle straight through her thumbnail. She was maybe nine years old. I don't know why she didn't faint right then. The needle went clear through with hardly any bleeding. Somehow my mother remained calm and managed to remove it. She cleaned her thumb with mercurochrome and put a big bandage on. It must have hurt a lot, but my sister was tough. I don't remember her crying much, except when she couldn't get her own way.

Back then, jeans were not permitted in school. It was a big event later in my senior year when we had a "dress-down" day. We could wear cut-off shorts and jeans, neither of which I had. Oh, yes—not even slacks were allowed for girls. We always wore skirts or dresses, and I had an old girdle with snaps for when I wore stockings. The girdle held in my tummy that was void of adipose fatty tissue. It stifled my breath and hampered my eating, and did nothing to improve my appearance. It was something we wore that did not make sense. I still hold that tight-fitting thing responsible for my lack of a flat stomach.

I was at a neighboring school that Friday in November, playing my flute with students planning to enter ensemble competition. When practice ended, we five kids that lived far away boarded a small van. We were enthusiastic, planning for the weekend, excited and nervous about how we would do in our upcoming performances. Someone said they had trouble finding time to practice. Another student declared that their family couldn't take listening to them braying on their clarinet for hours on end.

When I told them I practiced outside in the barn, they stared at me, then laughed. I explained that on warmer days I could rehearse for marching band going up and down my wide open front yard. I bragged how I didn't need to carry music because I had it all memorized.

THE STRONGEST BOND

We sat awhile chatting and wondered why the bus driver wasn't there yet. A teacher opened the back doors of the van, climbed in, and sat next to us. She was crying. "President Kennedy's been shot." Her chin trembled as she spoke with stuttered words. She was wringing her hands. I heard a student utter a soft cry. We asked a lot of questions. "Is he going to be okay? What will happen? Who will run the country? What will we do?" She answered as best she could, and reassured us. She said, "Go home to your families and watch the news. You'll be safe."

It made for a long and solemn ride. We all had questions, but instead we sat hushed, on our opposite-facing padded bench seats. We looked past each other's eyes and fixed our attention out the windows, lost in our own worries as we watched the countryside go by. I was anxious to get home, and with each student's departure, came a strange and fearful dread. I'd told myself that this year I would not be afraid of anything. Now I doubted if I could keep that promise.

Being the last stop on the route, after an hour or more, I arrived home and waved goodbye to the van driver. Entering the driveway, I walked with slow steps toward our small home. It was a quiet, surreal day. By four o'clock that afternoon we were all sitting fixed in front of the TV, watching and listening in disbelief. We were not a family engaged in politics, and so my opinions about what happened were limited, but my feelings of defeat and thoughts of death ran deep.

The images we saw and discussions we had about what happened that afternoon landed a punch to my gut. I recognized the familiar, painful twinges that made my jaw clench tight and my breath short and shallow. Thoughts of my mother's death came on with a fierceness of missing her. My newly found feelings of independence dwarfed my emotional state that cried for her to come back. It was not fair that she had died, and now our president was

A BOXING BOND

killed. He, like my mother was good, young, with a family. He had been our hope for better lives, and so had she.

I plunged ahead into my classes, determined to be self-assured and not afraid. The days passed. Snow arrived without much fanfare, but in time for an easier hunting season for my dad and his buddies. I wasn't thinking about boyfriends, but as luck had it, I met Danny through friends of my father's who lived a few miles from us just over the Pennsylvania border. He was a year older than I was, and joined the hunting group. He was skinny, tall, green-eyed, blond, and soft-spoken. We got along right away and began debating hunting. I had strong feelings about hurting animals even though it was made clear to me that it was to gain meat for the coming winter.

I also could not enjoy the chickens we killed by chopping off their heads and then watching them run feverishly around the yard, as if their brains didn't know that they were dead. And the pigs that were once our pets that we slaughtered made me retch at the thought of eating them. The gentle, beautiful, and graceful deer were shot with my father's own rifle and brought home as a prize that I had never wanted to see.

Our large vegetable garden yielded the foods I loved most. The only drawbacks were my green-stained hands from weeding, and the appearance of a passing snake that ambled near me while sitting in the potato patch.

In spite of Danny's involvement in hunting, I was very attracted to him and flourished with his attention. My father knew and trusted him; thus we were allowed to go out unescorted in his '57 Chevy, reveling in each other's company and above suspicion. By spring the weather was pleasant as we'd walk to meet each other halfway on the dirt road that ran between his home and mine. Apart from when I'd stop to pick roadside wildflowers, we'd hold hands, kicking up dust as we went along. I'd pluck the daisy petals one by one rhyming "he loves me, he loves me not" hoping the last petal would be "he loves me."

When I visited his home, we spent most of our day in the finished basement that had a ping-pong and pool table. I sent those white plastic ping-pong balls into the air skillfully at him and wildly about the room in absolute delight. I held my own with pool, but he was more mathematically adept at figuring angles, so he sunk the pool balls into the pockets more often.

We'd hike into the woods on evenings when we could stay out longer. The tree house was a chosen place for us to be by ourselves. Filled with youthful infatuation, we shared a sleeping bag, coming close enough to rub elbows and knees, half-dressed in a pinch-and-tickle match.

As the year went on and we became more serious about each other, he invited me to his senior prom. Those were lighthearted days for us. We rode around in his Chevy listening to The Beach Boys, joined together in thoughts of green ocean waves, silver-sand beaches and "fun, fun, fun" lyrics that ran through our minds and flowed freely from our lips. It was a time of teenage freedom, a simpler phase for me as I moved toward making my own decisions without oversight or close scrutiny. I felt loved, and hidden in a bubble of contentment.

On a warm balmy evening in June, Danny arrived to pick me up for his prom. I opened my door to see him wearing a suit and bow tie, and looking a little nervous. I was in my full-flowing, long-skirted pink chiffon dress, with a white crocheted shawl across my shoulders. I gazed lovingly into his eyes while bunches of butterflies flittered in my stomach.

With one hand hiding behind his back, he was prepared as he proudly presented a purple orchid on a wristlet band of pink ribbon. He placed it securely on my thin waiting wrist. The night was magic. We danced in awkward back and forth moves across the gym floor

A BOXING BOND

as sparkling lights twirled about the room, weaving between and around us. I was on top of the world. Someone loved me.

The summer of 1964 with Danny was ending, and with it the light happy-hearted moments that had beat wonderfully within me. I had one more year of high school. He and his parents had plans for him to attend Penn State in the fall. I was left too soon without him, with hopes that he would return to me the following summer. But as is with many things, they do not remain as they are at any given time. They have their place in life and they change their pace as the days pass.

We spoke over that year, vowing to keep in touch with each other, and when he came back after his first year at college he was grown up, mature, and more handsome. His future held so much that was planned, secure, and already underway. I didn't belong in his world anymore; nor did he fit in mine. I wasn't settled enough to see a future ahead like he could. I was barely able to navigate high school and home duties. Still being shaped by life's storms, I was inexperienced, lacking exposure to the larger world.

Along the road in spring the dandelions sing, lowly near the ground below their chorus reaches high, and when they shed their yellow glow, floating strands of seeded white fly into the air, granting wishes everywhere.

9

A MASTER PLAN

I asked the construction worker, "This road ends in a 'Y,' so which way should I go?" He shrugged his shoulders and answered, "When I don't know which road to take, I call on the one who created the master plan."

THE PAST FEW YEARS OF high school had dragged along until all of a sudden it was my senior year, and I was set to graduate at seventeen. I was feeling grown-up, preparing to be on my own. I had a job every other weekend as a nurse's aide at the hospital. I'd purchased my first set of new clothes with my own money: a burgundy straight skirt and a pink oxford long-sleeved blouse. It was the first time I could choose my clothes instead of being subjected to my cousins' styles, even though their clothes were nice. In fact, I went to an apparel store and shopped—a novel experience for me. I proudly walked the halls of school, head up, back straight, books in the bend of my arm, looking smart and studious with my brand-new outfit.

I was ahead of my peers, more assured and independent when it came to everyday living. And like my brother John, I began contributing to the household. I gave the extra money I'd saved that was tucked in my dresser drawer to my dad when he asked. Temporary episodes of insecurity and fears kept me doubting about which way to head in my life. I knew I had to finish high school, and I already had a job. I was using a map with symbols pointing away from where I was, but not to where I wanted to be. It felt like I was being spun around in an open field of crop circles.

I'd traveled an uncertain tangled path that stretched out before me when my mother became sick. It took me through a passage of realistic problem-solving interlaced with wishes and make-believe. My progress was slow, but when the days were sunny and the expanse of sky above greater than the earth below, I became optimistic and engaged in escapist mind games of levitation, positive I could lift my feet inches from the ground to stand midair. I was determined to pull the tablecloth out from under dishes without moving them, and actually succeeded a few times, but I could not concentrate enough to bend a spoon using my mental powers.

My spirit was consoled with divine visions that appeared several times in bright iridescent rays of light in the corner of my room near my dresser—the same place my mother's light visited me twice after she died. I was intimately in touch with a spiritual creative force that moved closer to me whenever I became distant. No matter which direction I took at that "Y" in the road, He was waiting there with a master plan. Regrettably, more often than not, I was impatient—sure that I knew best.

A pattern had emerged in the years after my mother died. Its design was filled with leftover tears and laughter from my journey. It cried out to me, "Run—escape to the other side; you can make it, it will be better." If I could draw a picture of it, flowers, trees, and weeds would cover the page. It was not a straight path that I'd followed in the days I agonized, hanging on to loss and holding out for hope that I could forge my own destiny.

What is faith? This is a question so many people ask. It was a question I never had asked. But when I was about eight years old, I questioned, "What is death? Where do you go when you die?" I was at that time fascinated with death, determined to make sense of it, after one of our neighbors died unexpectedly. I recall thinking that if I could die and come back, I would know where he went and what it was like. Not many people could answer my questions about death in a way that I could understand. Yet I had no doubt that God made me, and I found great consolation in all of nature's creations. My faith accepted the greatest mysteries, and I was convinced there was no limit to what God could do.

As I stood beside my mother, this time she wore a silky blue nightgown. Her face was calm, her body still when I looked down into her coffin. Everyone was fixed in long-faced stares. What did these gawking people want me to do? "What is death?" I'd asked before, and now again at fourteen. She wasn't here anymore. I needed to know why she had to die. Tears held tight to my throat and washed my feelings like a river coursing deep and wild.

Later, her coffin dressed with flowers flowing over the top and down the side was carried up the church steps and through the tall baroque wooden doors. The men beside it bore serious strained faces that matched their somber steps. Into the center aisle and to the front altar they marched, and placed the coffin atop a stand for all to see its morose beauty.

The haunting fragrance of frankincense emanated from the censer as the long-robed priest followed behind, swinging it methodically left and then right on its chain. The air filled with a smoky mist that weaved its way among us in an attempt to heal the sadness bound tightly in our hearts.

Our family rode chauffeur-driven through the streets, past houses and up the cemetery hill in the funeral parade for my mother. My father, with his face wet from crying, was sitting next to me. He asked in an angry grief-stricken tone, "What's the matter with you? Why don't you cry? Didn't you love your mother?" Instantly I was engulfed with vexing swells that pushed tears unrelenting down my face, tears that did not leave me until her coffin was lowered into the earth before my unbelieving eyes. The time went slowly past, and the answer to my question "What is death?" was added to the list of all the great mysteries that I had accepted.

As a young child, I loved to sit near my mother in our Catholic church on the perfectly honed dark wood benches. My sister was on one side of her and I was on the other. My brothers, impeccable gentlemen, escorted us into the pew first and placed themselves on the end in their protective stance.

The stained-glass windows lined the walls and filtered the sun's rays through the images of Christ and His disciples depicted in the Stations of the Cross. My head bowed, I soaked in the colorful warm light, and my heart was penetrated by the splendor of reverence surrounding me.

My mother was the portrait of a saint. Her character was stately, pure, and full of peace. Her faith exuded from every action: an infinite faith, evident even when she held our hands and spoke in whispers in an attempt to quell our incessant questions and erratic squirming.

In front of our lined pews beneath an ornate altar of statues, the low light of candles flickered through rows of red holders. The priest spoke in lilting phrases and lifting chords of song, a flowing, rambling verbiage I didn't recognize. It was Latin. Behind and far above our heads in a balcony, choir voices floated down covering us with soprano notes of Alleluia. It held me fixed, almost hushing my movements, entranced in the ebb and flow of sounds that flooded my ears. It turned my attention inward, and much to my mother's dismay, alternately it turned my head upward, as I looked around to the balcony from where the music came. I wanted to see the choir members that were tucked back behind the tall closed-railing banister. After the service, if my mother stopped to talk, I'd run up the stairs at the back of the church and lean over that barrier. Standing high above, looking down, ideas, imaginings and lyrics of song kept vigil inside my head.

A MASTER PLAN

Until about twelve years of age, I was determined to be a nun, profoundly influenced by the solitude and comforts of church with my mother's resilient spiritual guidance. It was the entrance of significant feelings toward boys as I entered my teens that led me to think of other occupations.

I would fall asleep nights kneeling at my bed while rolling the rosary beads between my fingers and repeating the prayers over and over. I directed them to God and the Virgin Mary, whose voices responded by pulsating into my waiting consciousness, imparting a knowing. Its wisdom was not concrete like my five senses. In fact, it was the dulling of these physical senses that ushered in its language, in the silence. Often after a sleepless night, a plethora of intuitive messages would etch themselves into my being.

The world was before me as never before. I would make my own road away from where I was. Not alone in this undertaking, I carried an irrepressible spirit. The fears I'd faced before made me able to go bravely. My wildest longings were yet to be fulfilled. All I needed to do was finish high school. My future was a step away.

My family was a part of me that could never be replaced. I made the decision to leave them behind and to keep them always. I went forward without consulting the Master's plan to become a part of another person's world—someone I hardly knew. I believed the magic of love was like the wave of a wizard's wand that could transform me from a scullery maid to Cinderella when the prince placed upon my foot the glass slipper of happy-ever-after. I didn't realize that the loves I'd lost had seared burning holes into my heart, branding me unlovable, incapable of loving myself, not feeling worthy of the very love I sought. I was empty, needy, and like the moon, I would travel through many phases before becoming full again.

10

WINGS

"Having tired of the negative words—she laid them down. Being finished with the weighted boots, she burned them. Touching a feather to her tears, she slipped on her wings, turned to her sky—and flew." Unknown

RAINDROPS, LIKE TEARDROPS, ARE KNOWN to fall at will, and pay no attention to desires for a sunny outcome. Today is a rainy day such as that, the Friday before Memorial Day weekend when many people make their plans to get away. It's odd they want to escape on a day that takes them back to reminisce. The temperature has dropped into the forties. A bright white layer of atmosphere hides just behind a gray dreary haze, pretending the sun will shine through. A solitary elderly neighbor walks with slow plodding steps, following behind his push mower, ignoring the dense wet grasses that fold without cutting beneath the blades.

Sometimes remembering makes me flare up with love seeping into every part of me, and other times it leaves me melancholy, empty, alone like a howling wolf on a moonlit night. Today my mind summons the seeping kind of love that floats like a butterfly over a flower bush and into my waiting thoughts.

Cold nights bring with them warm memories of our family as we'd shout in unison, "I smell chili and cherry pie." Dad would hum to himself and smile, "The pie is in the oven and the chili is on the stove. Almost ready, come and get it!" My father took great pride in fixing his special recipe for chili and making homemade cherry pie for dessert: his favorites, and our prized meal! A simple place setting of chili and buttered saltine crackers on a cold winter's night gave my mother a welcome reprieve from cooking. She sat resting, relishing the food's aromas, not needing to do a thing but eat as the scents floated in a circle around our dining room table.

After we finished our big bowls of chili, leaving just enough room for pie, my brothers would pipe in with "Where's the ice cream?" Teasing, my father would say, "Oh no! I forgot the ice cream!" But we all knew better. My brother John would jump to the freezer and pull out the carton of vanilla to pass along for each of us to scoop over our sweet steaming pie.

Hot summer days bring memories of when my father drove his big red tractor, with the small wheels at the front in the middle, and huge wheels at the rear. When I was a little girl, I'd sit up on a back wheel fender and ride with him across hay fields and down gullies. The big tires marked spaces where they pressed heavy, pulling up the ground from under the grass, causing dirt to swirl about us as we rumbled along. The small front tires rolled out over the weeds in the center, smoothing down perfect green tracks. The tractor bumped and leaned, crossing the rocky shallow stream where water splashed on my feet and up my pants.

We climbed hills with slow loud chugging thuds from shifting gears. For fear of sliding off, I'd jump down, grabbing hold of the wide rim around the tractor seat. My dad's floppy hat sprang up and down as he sat tall, bouncing high, looking carefree, whistling into the buggy hot sultry air. Pesky gnats darted at my face and clung to my sweaty skin, but I loved with entirety riding with him on that tractor. He didn't have to say how much he cared. He took me with him into a place we shared, together in that quiet universe between us.

Those little-girl days fell away without as much as a fond

goodbye to let me know I had grown up, and out of the cocoon of innocence that held me in a soft net of fine spider silk. I was almost eighteen, at my high school senior prom, without a date. I lined up against the wall with the girls, and looked across the room to where, like us, the boys were doing the same.

But unlike us, they didn't need to sit demurely or pose, appearing to model, while secretly wilting for fear that they would never be asked to dance. Some of the boys milled about, hands in their pockets, looking like young men, while other boys were skinny, shy, and peered out from under thick eyeglasses hiding their handsome faces, which one day would emerge and demand to be shaved regularly.

As I stood without a sound, hugging the wall behind me, I studied my pink flowing prom dress, the one I'd worn the year before while I whirled around in dance, held by my date, at his senior prom. I felt a quiet confidence, evoking the memory of how I once was chosen and adored.

The seat next to where I stood was freed up after the girl occupying it was asked to dance. Not having the best-fitting shoes, my feet sighed with relief as I lowered into the empty chair. A refrain of romantic love notes inspired couples to pair up, dancing close. I wished for time to go faster, they seemed to move in embrace as if the night and the music would never end. I welcomed the chance to sit and appear less conspicuous among the few of us remaining, whose presence was not required at center stage.

When the girls returned who didn't stay on the gym floor awaiting the next song, I stood, relinquishing my seat for them to rest their feet. The tempo picked up as the waltz waned and popular melodies with a faster beat filled the room. Fewer couples took to the floor and some girls danced with each other.

A boy with slicked-back greasy hair, a crooked bowtie, and wrinkled slacks approached and asked me to dance. I felt bad for him, as I gestured soundlessly with a negative shake of my head, politely declining, not wanting to hurt his feelings. He walked away, shoulders drooped. As I watched him retreat, not looking ahead, a deep resonant voice caught my ear. A young man with olive skin, dark hair, green eyes, and a broad smile drew near, requesting, "Would you like to dance?" Taken in by his charming appearance, I didn't think twice as I sweetly replied, "Yes, I would."

The Beatles tune "I Saw Her Standing There" played as we moved toward the center of the gym, hand in hand. My heart skipped a beat, and pounding loud enough for him to hear it, kept pace with the lyrics as my feet barely touched the floor. Our story was being told that night as we joined hands, our days moving one into the other, that summer of 1965.

I recall a day not long after my mother died in 1962. Feeling especially needy of love, I tried to cuddle my parakeet, Tweety Bird, when he angrily bit my finger nearly drawing blood. It was not unusual for him, considering that he was noisy, mean, and unpredictable. Aside from that, I was determined to tame him into loving me.

For some reason his bite sent me into an intense rage, as I grabbed tightly with both hands, squeezing his tiny neck, attempting to strangle him. I bolted to the front door, held him in one hand, opened it wide, and stood threatening to send him away into the great outdoors. I screamed, "You rotten no-good mean bird. Why don't you let me love you? You can fly away for all I care! I hate you. I hate you."

Just then, I loosened my grip, and Tweety flew off into the open countryside. I was so stunned, I raced after him calling, "Come back, come back—I'm sorry!" but it was too late and he was too fast. Hysterical, I ran to the house to get my brother, crying, "Help, help, Tweety flew away. I'll never get him; he's gone forever. We'll never find him in the woods!"

WINGS

Art ordered, "Stop crying—we'll get him." My sister came to help too. It was autumn and more leaves were on the ground than on the trees.

We began systematically checking each tree leading from our house in the direction he flew. I had almost given up, when we spotted a bright green color atop a bare branch. It was Tweety! My brother had a long-handled net we'd used to chase bats that fluttered into our house. He raised it slowly, and with one fast swoop, Tweety was caught. I was exhausted from the ordeal, but thrilled and relieved to have him back.

This time, loosely held in my hands, he seemed weak and defenseless and I feared he was sick from being out in the cold. Tenderly, I returned him to the safety of his cage. I fussed, saying, "I am sorry, so sorry. I didn't mean to let you go, my baby, sweet baby bird," as if now he would allow me to pet him, and forgive me for trying to wring his neck.

Those summer days quickly gave way to fall that fateful year when I turned eighteen. I was sure I'd met the man of my dreams at my senior prom. We'd graduated high school and began talking about getting married as I secretly planned my escape from home. It wasn't like I could tell my father about him. We didn't really talk like fathers and daughters do. I had no idea what would happen. I was afraid he would try to stop us. I couldn't gamble with what I envisioned as my only chance for love.

I was confined, like my Tweety Bird but unlike him, I was going to fly away and never be caged again. I was going to be free, high above it all. My flying dreams had increased, becoming more and more real. I would take wing; it was my turn to soar. In the night, I ascended traversing the sky, above buildings, trees, and the people walking below, my body horizontal, arms outstretched pointing ahead of me like Superman, but with a big "S" for Susan on my royal-blue shirt.

THE STRONGEST BOND

I kept a steady distance between myself and the ground, never dipping too low where a person could grab me, and never drifting too high, for fear of not getting back down. When flying weather was stormy, I persevered, straining to see through rain, dark clouds, lightning, and snow to follow the thin bands of road wherever I was headed that night.

The day was like any other late in autumn, fresh with crisp apples, falling leaves, and changing skies. Except this day, when my father dropped me off for work at the hospital, my knapsack was packed with necessities and a change of clothes. "See you later," I called as I left, knowing later I would arrive at a different place in time. I wasn't coming back home—not until I was stronger, protected, and married. No longer would I have to endure wordless pain suspended in the air that permeated the rooms of our home with the loss of my mother and the loss of the loving father that I once knew...a father that now oppressed my spirit that longed to be free, and my heart that only wanted him to love me the way I loved him.

EPILOGUE

MOST FAMILIES CLAIM A SENSE of permanence in their homes. After being away, they return to sit in a familiar chair, look out of a window, or stand at the kitchen sink. It is where their lives began, and they say, "I lived here, and so-and-so lived next door. Dad and I, and Mom or a sister and brother did this, or that."

They gather together, stirring a pot of memories to savor over dinner. Reinforcing the belonging, and reconnecting with the past when they were eighteen, and all of life was ahead of them. Their dreams were filled with going-to-dos. But all too soon, the I-wish-I'd-done-that's showed up in their rearview mirrors.

As I returned home, where it began for me, I found goldenrods, high bushes, and towering trees covering the front yard. The thick green wood's I'd walked as a child floated over the land like a painting. I descended into a path that dipped among the weeds, down the hill to the left where our house once stood, and to the right toward the barn. The high wind-swept grasses held me back as I searched for a remnant of the tiny house that I had embraced.

I gazed at the barn, jutting salient up through the overgrowth in spite of its rubble of stone and heaped-up scraps of wood. It had once rose up tall and steady, bursting with sounds of horses, cats, dogs, chickens, and cows. As I approached, it spoke to me of revival, hoping another family like ours would come and love it back to life.

The mailbox just off the road told everyone where we lived,

and who we were. It was there, on school days, that my sister, my brothers, and I waited for the bus. When the driver pushed open its wide door, we climbed the steep steps, and entered into our yellow bubble of friends.

My book, *The Strongest Bond*, ended when I'd left home at eighteen full of dreams. After turning its last page, the blank whiteness stared at me, incredulous, expecting more. Before long, my second book appeared with love stories from my past. I had learned that we love each other imperfectly. It is the way it's meant to be. And sometimes, no matter how much we love someone, it's not enough.

CPSIA information can be obtained at www.ICGtesting.com
Printed in the USA
BVOW11s1106020714

357948BV00002B/8/P